Twin Flames

Discover The Mythology of Soul Mates and the Twin Flame Union, Disunion, and the Reunion

by Andrew M. Parsons
http://www.andrewmparsons.com

Table Of Contents

INTRODUCTION

CHAPTER 1: THE MYTHOLOGY OF A TWIN FLAME

CHAPTER 2: THE MYTHOLOGY OF A SOUL MATE

CHAPTER 3: HOW TO KNOW AND TELL THE DIFFERENCE BETWEEN A TWIN FLAME AND A SOUL MATE

CHAPTER 4: HOW TO KNOW SOMEONE IS YOUR TWIN FLAME

CHAPTER 5: THE UNION, DISUNION, AND THE REUNION

CHAPTER 6: SEARCHING FOR YOUR TWIN FLAME/SOUL MATE AND THE LAW OF ATTRACTION

CONCLUSION

CHECK OUT MY OTHER BOOKS

INTRODUCTION

We are always looking for that one person who will complete us. Someone that will make us realize that we are never meant to be alone in this world. We all have a twin soul, or if not that, then a soul mate. The problem is, we fail to look for them. Sometimes, we have found them, but we ignore them.

In our busy life, we often take for granted the makings of the universe. We become so absorbed with our careers, our business, and our dreams, that we fail to stop for a moment, and bask in the knowledge that there is someone out there, willing to accept us for who we are, regardless of what we've been through. In this book, you will learn about the mythologies of Twin Flames and Soul Mates. You'll learn these are part of a soul group and how they are here to teach life lessons. What are their differences? Should finding our twin flame mean that we have completed our purpose here on earth? What about our soul mates? What can we do to initiate the process of finding them? What processes will we undergo once we have found them?

If you're ready to embark on a soulful journey, then please proceed in learning about the origins of twin flames.

Thank you for purchasing this book. I hope you enjoy it!

© Copyright 2015 by Accredited Solutions, Inc. - Twin Flames- All rights reserved.

This document is geared towards providing exact and reliable information in regards to the topic and issue covered. The publication is sold with the idea that the publisher is not required to render accounting, officially permitted, or otherwise, qualified services. If advice is necessary, legal or professional, a practiced individual in the profession should be ordered.

- From a Declaration of Principles which was accepted and approved equally by a Committee of the American Bar Association and a Committee of Publishers and Associations.

In no way is it legal to reproduce, duplicate, or transmit any part of this document in either electronic means or in printed format. Recording of this publication is strictly prohibited and any storage of this document is not allowed unless with written permission from the publisher. All rights reserved.

The information provided herein is stated to be truthful and consistent, in that any liability, in terms of inattention or otherwise, by any usage or abuse of any policies, processes, or directions contained within is the solitary and utter responsibility of the recipient reader. Under no circumstances will any legal responsibility or blame be held against the publisher for any reparation, damages, or monetary loss due to the information herein, either directly or indirectly.

Respective authors own all copyrights not held by the publisher.

The information herein is offered for informational purposes solely, and is universal as so. The presentation of the information is without contract or any type of guarantee assurance.

The trademarks that are used are without any consent, and the publication of the trademark is without permission or backing by the trademark owner. All trademarks and brands within this book are for clarifying purposes only and are the owned by the owners themselves, not affiliated with this document.

Chapter 1: The Mythology Of A Twin Flame

The concept of twin flames is not a new age farce, like so many people are led to believe. One of the first texts where the concept of twin souls is mentioned is in the **Symposium**, a philosophical writing authored by Plato. Plato here describes a speech made by another ancient wise guy, the Greek playwright Aristophanes, which some scholars label as pure satire. Under that thick crust of sarcasm, hides the ancient errors in our human nature, understanding of love, unity and divine connection. This ancient text speaks of a creation myth, one that is forgotten, or simply left out.

The Story...

According to Aristophanes' speech, the ancient man once had four legs, four arms, one head with two faces. Their bodies were roundly shaped, and all humans had two sets of genitals. Some were male, some female and others – androgynous (having male and female genitalia). The males were said to be descendants of the sun, the females originated from the earth, and the androgynous were the offspring of the moon, having genitals of the both genders because the moon was the loving child of the sun and earth. Having multiple limbs, these humans were able to run fast, stand up straight, fold on all fours and run on their back, just as fast as they would run on their front. Knowing their power and capabilities, they grew arrogant and pretentious. Soon enough, they planned to overthrow the Gods on Olympus. The Gods were scared of their power, and they didn't like the way their humans rebelled. So Zeus developed a plan, to keep them occupied. At first, he wanted to destroy them with thunderbolts, but that would have left the gods without offerings, admiration and honors. He thought of a better plan– to cut them in half. So from one human, he made two, separating one soul in two different bodies.

Since Zeus split them in half, each one of them continued to long for the lost part. That is the ancient explanation of why some people are attracted to the same gender, while others connect with people of the opposite gender. That is the origin of the saying that we are always searching for our other half and the feeling of oneness when we find that special someone. It may be just a story, an ironic attempt on Aristophanes part, to describe his fellow humans as species that got punished for making themselves known to duality, polarity and separatism. Centuries later, the joke is still on us. We still find ourselves separate from everyone else. We divide ourselves into groups and think of other human beings as isolated entities.

The Journey of Twin Souls

In today's new age philosophies, this concept is extended and taken as a crucial part of spiritual growth and awakening. Today too, the twin soul concept illuminates our creation, the way we got here and what are we doing on the physical plane. Some people believe everything on earth comes from a distinct source. Many Eons ago, the source dispatched sparks of its own divinity. These sparks are thought to inhabit everything there is in the universe. One group is said to have traveled to the earth and in time, they became the first inhabitants of our planet. They traveled through the celestial, angelic, spiritual, astral, mental and etheric plane, until they became the physical manifestation we are today. At the beginning of the planet, the souls settled in stones, crystals and minerals. Later they inhabited the vegetation kingdom, where each group resided in different species. Every orchid that grew on earth, for example, held bits of one soul, every branch of poison ivy shared a different soul, and each tree was the home of another soul. All souls sent from the source inhabited every living plant there was at the time.

When the animal kingdom appeared, the souls transferred their energy there. One soul was now divided into each animal, which is why the animals bred between their own species. The souls at the time did not have self awareness, each soul could only find the difference between "them" and "us". As the animals reproduced, their collective soul was either divided or incarnated, so that every newborn could identify with its own species.

When from animals we developed into humans, we no longer stayed within our group. As our minds progressed and developed, we separated even further. We mixed with other souls, usually out of convenience. As time passed by, one collective soul was scattered throughout the world, until each soul was divided in two parts, twin flames. Some may reunite with there other half while other may not. Those who do are souls we call **enlightened,** because they recognize themselves as one soul in two bodies. When this happens, and the two "half souls" clear up their karmic debt, many believe that when they die, their soul waits at the border of the celestial realm. Often times, they choose to be reborn with the purpose to help other twin souls find each other. These are usually people with great personal power, serenity and steadfast wisdom.

Chapter 2: The Mythology Of a Soul Mate

We have heard the fairy tales of the sleeping beauty, who could only be woken up by the kiss of her one true love, her soul mate. But the concept of soul mates is also accepted in many, if not all religions.

In Christianity, soul mates are described in both, the Old and New Testament. In the Old Testament, God creates Adam and Eve, Adam from dust and Eve from one of his ribs. In the New Testament, the connection between the soul mates is described as God given. A type of bond that other people should not try to break. According to the gospel of Matthew, a man and a woman that are joined in marriage are no longer two, but one flesh. The rabbinical literature goes even further, and describes Adam as androgynous, from whom God made his companion, Eve. Even today, in Judaism this concept is still present, and young Jewish people are encouraged to date until they find their soul mate, or ***ezerk'negdo***. In Hinduism, the concept of soul mates merges with the one of twin souls, where it is written that the soul, once it becomes conscious of itself, divides into a male and female part, only to be joined again and experience the power of divine love.

The Story

Nevertheless, one of the oldest soul mate stories is found in Egyptian mythology. The connection between Osiris and Isis started in the womb. They were born as twins, but they were also lovers, who conceived a child, named Horus. Osiris's brother, Set, was jealous of their love and divine connection, so he kidnapped and killed Osiris and cut him into 14 pieces. But their eternal devotion to one another doesn't end there, as with other soul mates alike. Isis later gathered the 14 pieces and brought her brother and lover back to life. But these two love birds are not the only soul mates in Egyptian mythology. Osiris's mother and father were soul mates as well. Even though his mother, the earth goddess Geb, was married to the sun god, Ra, she was in love with Nut, the sky god. Ra didn't like their love, and tried to separate them by putting the air god Shu between them. They were separated during the day by the sun god, but the sky god would sneak in and lay over the earth goddess during the night, which was the reason why the night was dark, according to the Egyptian beliefs. Ra ordered his wife to cease giving birth throughout the year, of 360 days. Nut asked for help from the god of wisdom, so he stole some light from the moon, which at the time was just as bright as the sun, and produced light for another 5 days in the year. That gave Geb a chance to obey her husband's wishes and be with her loved one again.

Stories about holy connections between entities have been present in many other religions and mythologies. P'amKu in Chinese theology describes the inseparable energies of yin and yang, the Sumerian texts speak about the joining of the god Anu and the goddess Ki, the Maori mythology had their own story of soul mates, named Papa and Rangi. Every time, the soul mates stay together regardless of adversities, enemies and physical distances, which is the true purpose of the soul mates.

Chapter 3: How To Know And Tell The Difference Between a Twin Flame And a Soul Mate

Adam, Eve, and Lilith

We all know the story about Adam and his soul mate Eve, but before Eve, Adam had a twin soul that got away. In the Bible, she is described as an evil demon that roams the earth looking for newborns and takes their souls. Not many people know that the bible had scripts, which were never included in the Holy Book. According to these scripts, Adam's first wife was Lilith. God made Lilith from dust, just as he made Adam. They were the first people in heaven, until Adam decided he's the more important one. Lilith did not like the way her loved one tried to marginalize her, so she tried to make him realize that since God made them equal, he should not try to take away her power and importance. Adam disregarded her position, after which she escaped the heaven and roved into the deep sea. After a while, Adam got lonely, so God made another woman for him, this time using one of his ribs. He did so to make Adam realize that even though she is different from him, she is still a part of him and he should respect her. Later in the Bible, Lilith is believed to appear again, taking the form of a snake and convincing Eve into taking the forbidden fruit.

The Difference Between a Soul Mate and a Twin Soul

Whether you believe this story to be true or not, it is still a representation of the difference between soul mates and twin souls. Adam's soul mate was Eve, because she complemented him. Lilith was Adam's twin soul, because she was made from the same dust as her male counterpart, they shared the same design, and God gave her her soul the same way he gave Adam his, using his breath.

Both Lilith and Eve were a part of Adam's soul group. A soul group is a group of infinite beings of consciousness who help us learn life lessons. The majority of individuals we have or have had in our lives have been with us in previous incarnations and have spent the majority of time with us in the ethereal realms. While we're on the "other side", we make agreements with our soul groups to meet at some juncture in our Earthbound lives (or any other place of incarnation, it doesn't have to be Earth).

Adam was to learn equality and balance from Lilith. Having failed to learn this from Lilith, he was able to learn it from Eve. See, both were a part of his life and if a lesson is not mastered, it will be relived lifetime after lifetime with different soul beings until it is accomplished.

The differences between a soul mate and a twin flame are many. You will instantly feel warmth in your heart when you meet a soul mate, but you may not always like your twin soul. Regardless, we all want to find the one by our way of choice. So when you eventually meet your twin flame or soul mate, you may not recognize it as such. You may have strong feelings about the person, but you may not identify them as love, or even friendship. It depends largely on your level of spirituality and the complexity of your karmic debt. The longer the soul group has stayed together, the easier it will be for each individual soul in it to recognize each other throughout their incarnations. If you have been forced to marry people from a different soul group, many times throughout your past lives, you may not be able to connect to your groups as easily. Your group may have been advancing, collecting earthly knowledge and wisdom, while you and your twin flame, soul mate are stuck on earth trying to find each other. The physical distance between you is not at all important, because our energy is always leading us towards them.

Everyone Has a Purpose

Everyone you meet has a message to share with you. When you have a negative experience with someone, the person may be a lost soul from another soul group. There are no bad or evil soul groups. Because we all come from the same source of light and divine energy, we are all little specks of godliness. We may mistakenly take someone for granted, not appreciate the gift they grant us just by being a part of our life. We often times think that a past relationship that ended badly, is a mistake we should have calculated. In actuality, there are no such relationships. Even those who've wronged you, they did it so to show you another path. A jealous manipulative ex lover was there to show you just how valuable your current relationship is. Because of that emotional turmoil, you can now grow and value your current partner. That relationship, although toxic has made you evolve more and more into your true self which in turn magnetically shift you towards finding your twin flame.

Did you know that when you are ready to learn something, suddenly a teacher will appear? The same rule goes for soul mates and twins. When your soul is ready to meet your matching half, your matching half will appear. **You can't force the issue, but there are ways you can stimulate the process.** Pay attention to your feelings and your inner voice. We sometimes forget that our intuitive mind is stronger than logic and defies many rules of reason. You need to find that voice and let it speak. You know how sometimes you meet someone, and later you hear a song that reminds you of them, or watch a movie where some character resembles the person you've met? You have met those people for a reason and you should watch those relationships closely. They will certainly be of great value to you.

Our Soul Mates

The chances of meeting a soul mate are great and connecting to soul mates is effortless, easygoing and comfortable. You will feel the need to connect with them instantly, you will find them interesting and intriguing. The things they say will always be the things you are interested in, have knowledge in or experienced at some point. You will have similar views on the world and similar goals in life. Your moral values will be the same, or you will enthusiastically want to change yours to fit theirs.

You may find a handful of soul mates throughout your life, and they may not always be people. They might not be your lovers, or spouses, and you might only meet them once. You may not even meet them in person, but read their books, listen to their music, or connect with them through social networks. Regardless, the connection will last a lifetime. You will always be glad to welcome them into your life, and let them explore the world as they please. They are the kindred souls that have to travel around and gather information for the sake of your collective soul growth. They are the souls who will wait for you at the edge of this world to reconnect and travel back to your original source.

Our Twin Flame

The twin flame connection is far more complex, and will bring out the negative qualities we tend to overlook in individual selves. The revelations brought upon by a twin flame are what make this relationship uniquely valuable. The most visible similarity between you two will be your temperament.

You may be very different people, coming from different cultures, living in different eras and expressing yourselves in different ways. The spark in the flame is a bond and with this bond, you will always love each other unconditionally with the same energetic vigor. Your values and views may differ, and you may disagree on many levels. Both of you will likely carry baggage from your past relationships, emotional baggage you are otherwise unwilling to look over. But in this special bond, you will accept their past and be willing, frustrating as may be, to work through it and aid each other in evolving. Your experiences have been different, but they bring profundity to your relationship. The relationship will transform both of you and send you both on a new path. Once you've met your twin flame you are bound to be together, in this life and in the next.

Chapter 4: How To Know Someone Is Your Twin Flame

It Starts From Within

To be able to meet your twin flame, and recognize it, you need to work on yourself first. You need to think really hard about what made you the person you are today. Your mistakes, choices and goals, even if they proved to be wrong and misleading, they all happened because you wanted to become who you are today. Even if there's something you and your twin flame disagree on, you will always be able to see, or feel their perspective. They will always read your mind too, which may be gratifying, but it may also be disconcerting. So much so you may even part for a while. Your weakness may be their fort and vice verse. It is a balance of energy.

What Happens When We Meet Our Twin Soul?

Usually when we meet our twin souls, **a wave of energy** comes over us and hugs our energetic body. There is a shift in mood and puts us in a state of wonderment, dismay or quiet awe. This is because deep within the recesses of your spirit, you recognize this being from a prior lifetime. The energy that surrounds that person is familiar to us and we don't need to be empathetic in nature to absorb it. Their energy floats freely through us and ours through theirs.

When you come in contact with your twin flame, **the surrounding environment will shift**. Your surroundings will seem alive, regardless of where you are. A boisterous place will become a quiet lull. You will be utterly engrossed in each other that time and space disappears. You will feel one with everything around you, because your energetic body is reading out the energy exuding from your other half. This is a powerful force at work, which will make your life seem like a movie for a second.

Sometimes this is accompanied with *shivers* and *tingling*. You don't need to do anything special to connect with the other person, because your energies will do that without you. You can just stand still and let your energetic bodies merge. That is a feeling unlike anything else, unlike any love you've felt before. That is the home for your soul.

Be More Aware

Keep track of your surroundings. Be present in every moment. Is there anything out of the ordinary? How are the people around you acting, moving, speaking? Are they saying something your heart finds familiar? Do you want to turn around without having anything to look at that particular direction? Pay attention if something suddenly seems strange, even more if those incidents layer on top of each other.

You and your twin soul are one child of the universe and it needs you together. It is a divine design and you are an important piece of the puzzle. When you are about to meet, the universe will send you signs for you to notice and bring you closer together. These common occurrences or as many may say, coincidences are actually synchronicity. Synchronicity is the simultaneous occurrence of events that are significantly related and serve as guided messages from our soul group on the other side. Repetitive events, symbols or numbers serve as hints that we are on the right path and with the right person.

Not everyone is fortunate enough to have their twin flame in their immediate environment. Although, if you have met in a previous life, chances are great you will be reincarnated closer and closer in each lifetime. You need to stay open to the possibilities and follow your instincts. What made you daydream about visiting Paris all of the sudden? You may be drawn to a particular destination, even though there's nothing there that may spark your interests, hobbies or lifestyle. Let that inner intuition guide you, because sometimes even the wrong trains may take you to the right place. Heed the messages your mind is sending you. We are a physical manifestation and being physically alive in a world of societies, we have been conditioned to discard the intangible or in this case spiritual data. Because of this, we have become numb and fail to sense other dimensions and energies. That's where our subconscious minds come into play. Keep records of the images your mind sends while you are talking to someone. Not the images related to the conversation you are having, but isolated images. Something you can't relate to the current engagement. Do you all of a sudden get a hint of what your life together could be? Do you imagine yourself happy with them, holding hands, kissing, even raising kids? These images don't even need to be of the two of you, they can be old images your brain collected from movies, daydreaming, or wishful thinking. In other words, your brain may send you a glimpse of heaven.

Finally, you will see how **other people react to your connection**. When you are with your twin flame, your bond is magnetically bright and inviting. Do you find others just looking at the both of you? It is because the energetic love is so pure others are just in awe with your energy. That kind of energy is noticeable and quite desired. Your union is inspiring and others will yearn to find their twin flame.

Consider yourself quite fortunate if you believe you have reunited with your twin flame because when two twins join their flames, it will ever keep burning into solid coals of love.

Chapter 5: The Union, Disunion, And The Reunion

Union is easy...

We made it sound so easy until now, leading you to believe that when you meet your twin flame, your lives will be sunshine and rainbows. But in reality, things may become complicated. **The likelihood of meeting your twin flame is great**, but you may not always like what you see. When you meet your twin soul, you are actually meeting yourself. What you see may not be pleasant, if you haven't nurtured your soul. Your spiritual awareness may need an upgrade in order for you to recognize a twin flame.

You may have been hurt and broken many times, so you've lost your faith in pure love. You may have been raised to believe that it's better to be with someone who's good on paper, rather than someone who's good for you in general. You may have never known how it feels to be in awe in the eyes of pure love. You need to work on your own spiritual enlightenment in order to accept and enjoy your other half.

Disunion

The physical beings we are in this lifetime are remnants of who we were in a past life. We all have positive and negative qualities. These negative aspects are karmic debris carried around from past lives.

For example, a previous life might have taught you that you can have anything you want, without paying your dues. You may have had partners who adored you and lavished you with gifts on a silver plate. This in turn makes you selfish, greedy and egotistical; believing everything you had is well deserved. These ego treatments don't serve your soul purpose, because even Plato knew that love is a give and take. So when you meet your twin flame, he will not see the flame behind the person swollen from gifts received and never having given back. He or she may see you as another red flag, decide to part and continue the search for their twin soul not knowing it is a divine plan and that they already found it.

The Dance-Resolving the Issues

It is your karma and you need to fix it. You need to clear up the way to your own flame, so that your twin won't get lost on the way. There isn't an "aha" moment, where your eyes sparkle and soft music plays in the background. Meeting your soul twin is not always pleasant, and may leave you with initial doubts. Yet the connection is authentic and pure. It is said that if you and your twin flame get on well from the first time you cross paths, you have already been together in your previous lives. Power struggles will be at play, since you both deliver the same type of energy. Many twin flames have deep lows and great highs. They hate each other, then love each other even more.

The richest aspect with this bond is the fact that both partners can sense what the other partner is feeling. They understand each other telepathically. You don't need too many words to describe your feelings because your partner is feeling the same. You and your other half will push each others buttons and test each others limits unlike anyone else. There is nothing antagonistic about this pattern, because in time, this emotional parlance will only enrich your bond.

Unlike soul mate relationships, this one will require effort towards progress. If you abandon your efforts, while your partner still has hopes for your life together, your lack of attention will almost certainly be considered a betrayal. Steps like these may lead to separation, even hatred. That is why, when you meet in your next life, you don't connect instantly. Same as Lilith and Adam. Once she turned her love to hate, she was demonized by an entire religion. Whichever the case, your twin vibration will stay entwined. The universe will remember your growth and reconnect you again. It may be in this lifetime or perhaps not until the next lifetime. Either way, if you have already met your twin flame, you have both achieved a state of heightened enlightenment. Enlightenment that will serve you during this life and in the next.

Reunion

The reunion is a coming home. On the border of the spiritual world, souls re-energize their energy, frequency and vibration with the rest of the twin souls from their soul group. There, the twin souls are no longer in two bodies. Their body is once again whole, as the source intended. Their energy is shared with the rest of the group, where knowledge of the earthly involvement is shared. Each soul knows the pains and sufferings, love and friendship every other soul experienced in their lives. Their last incarnation is a mutual decision to help the humankind reach a new level of consciousness.

Chapter 6: Searching For Your Twin Flame/Soul Mate And The Law Of Attraction

You and your twin flame or soul mate are a part of this universe. Your essence comes from the same place and will go back to the same place eventually. But to complete this final step, you need to let the universe help you find each other. The universe made you and your twin flame according to its most divine design, a miraculous automatic process that will eventually lead to energetic attraction. You need to clear the way for your own flame. The only way to do this is by loving yourself first. Respect and honor your individuality and embrace love for all things, including animals and nature. Once you do so, your love will resonate with your twin flame or soul mate's frequency which will then catapult a magnetic pull towards each other. The universe will know every one of your thoughts, actions and desires. Be sure to release only loving vibrations so your message.

Start by expressing gratitude for all your past relationships. Both, the positive and negative ones have brought you closer to your goals and desires. Thanks to them, now you have a pristine image of the things you want in a relationship and the things you don't want. Don't try to imagine the type of person you think you should end up with as this only leads to barriers. Regardless of their core and the purpose of the time you've been together, the universe has remembered the vibration of your joined energy. It already knows what kind of energy you need to be fulfilled, you just need to get rid of the restrictions you've put on your own happiness.

Instead of spending your time beating yourself up about the false judgments in your past relationship, **start thinking about the positive impetus they left on**

your life. They may have made you a better person, more patient or mature. They may have helped you get over a personal limitation, taught you to stand up for yourself or opened your eyes for some truth. If you keep feeling sorry for yourself or feel annoyed about your current situation, the universe will read your energy and give you a similar feedback. The universe doesn't understand your questions, it just reads your energy. It absorbs your vibrations and responds in the same manner.

Think of your mind as the most powerful gadget you own, with which you can communicate with a divine wish granting machine. There are no instructions on how to use this gadget, but it's completely controllable because it's your own. Pay attention of how you communicate with the universe. If you start your thoughts with "Why can't I have that girl" "Isn't there someone for me" or "I don't know how I'm going to find someone", the only messages you are sending out are "I can't" "There isn't" and "I don't". ***Make positive and constructive affirmations*** and you will see a difference. Change your patterns of thinking, because your thoughts will travel long distances. They are the echo of your desires, so try to send out the right ones.

Make a meditation out of it. If everything in the universe is made of energy, if you and your twin flame or soul mate share the same pulse, it will be easy to connect in another dimension. Close your eyes and imagine your own energetic body. It can be red, blue, green, shaped as a heart or a maple leaf.

Use your imagination to shape up your own energy and send it to the astral realm. You and your twin flame/soul mate have met there many times. That is why you are suddenly interested in this topic, and why you decided to read more about how to find them. Invite them with your welcoming thoughts.

Invite them to join you and help each other illuminate your paths towards one another. They want to meet you as well.

Let the universe know you are ready to receive what your soul has lost a long time ago. Don't hesitate and don't fear. There are no malicious gods and there is no pact with the devil. What you release you receive in return. It's as simple as that. Tell the universe you are waiting for your twin flame/soul mate to find you.

Find that seed of love you hide in the dark corners of your soul and give it a little light. Let that light grow and expand. Let it into your heart and multiply it. Once you let it grow, all you need to do is tend to it. Once you formulate your desires, every time you think of them, you are only watering the seeds of happiness and gratification. Pile up your body with loving feelings, thoughts of joy and ecstasy. It is the only recipe for happiness and satisfaction. You are well on your way.

Conclusion

Patience is key. Learn to embrace love within yourself and others. The truth is this, unless you are ready, nothing will happen.

Take peace in the knowledge that they are out there - your twin flame and your soul mate. They are waiting for you as well. Prepare yourself for them. Make their road to you easy by embracing love and your authentic self.

Go out, have fun, experience as much as you can (be it good or bad) while you are in the quest to find the people that will make you feel complete. After all, when you improve for your own sake, nothing but goodness will follow.

Finally, if you enjoyed this book, then I'd like to ask you for a favor, would you be kind enough to leave a review for this book on Amazon? It'd be greatly appreciated!

Thank you and good luck finding your twin flame and soul mate!

Andrew M. Parsons

Check Out My Other Books

Below you'll find some of my other books that are popular on Kindle as well. Simply type the book title in the search bar on Amazon.com and hit enter to check them out.

>>> Dating After Divorce: Discover Your Confidence and Overcome Your Dating Anxiety with the Simple Steps to Dating After Divorce

>>> Online Dating Tips for Beginners: Learn Valuable Dating Advice to Choose the Right Online Dating Websites to Find Love Online

>>>The Key To Online Dating For Men: Don't Be A Wimp! - Learn Key Online Dating Tips Guaranteed to Get Women to Respond

Also be sure to check out my personal blog at http://www.andrewmparsons.com.

Made in the USA
Las Vegas, NV
27 August 2022